CONVERTING FRACTIONS TO DECIMALS

VOLUME III

Math 5th Grade
Children's Fraction Books

Speedy Publishing LLC

40 E. Main St. #1156

Newark, DE 19711

www.speedypublishing.com

Copyright 2017

Hello! Welcome to Volume 3 in our series of practice books. A short discussion on how to Multiply and Divide the Fractions.

Are you ready to review what to do? Let's get started!

CONVERTING FRACTIONS TO DECIMAL FORM

A fraction sign – and the division sign ÷ are the same. So, whenever you see an equation like this, $\frac{1}{2}$.

It means: $\frac{1}{2}$ or $1 \div 2$

How to convert a fraction to decimal

➡ Divide the numerator by the denominator

$\frac{1}{2}$ ← Numerator

← Denominator

$$\frac{1}{2} = 1 \div 2 = 0.5$$

CONVERTING DECIMALS TO FRACTION FORM

How to convert a decimal to a fraction.

➡ Write down the decimal divided by 1, like this:

$$\frac{0.5}{1}$$

➡ Multiply both top and bottom by 10 for every number after the decimal point. If there are two digits after the decimal point, then use 100, if there are three then use 1000 and so on.

$$\frac{0.5 \times 10}{1 \times 10} = \frac{50}{100}$$

➡ Reduce to lowest term.

$$\frac{50}{100} = \frac{25}{50} = \frac{1}{2}$$

Okay! It's time to practice
what you have learned.

Have fun learning with
these cool fraction and
decimal activities!

Enjoy!

MULTIPLYING FRACTIONS

Multiply the fractions and convert the answers in Decimal form.

Multiply the fractions and convert the answers in Decimal form.

1) $\dfrac{3}{5} \times \dfrac{7}{2} =$

2) $\dfrac{2}{4} \times \dfrac{5}{2} =$

3) $\dfrac{2}{3} \times \dfrac{11}{3} =$

4) $\dfrac{1}{2} \times \dfrac{7}{4} =$

5) $\dfrac{1}{2} \times \dfrac{11}{4} =$

6) $\dfrac{8}{5} \times \dfrac{3}{4} =$

7) $\dfrac{14}{5} \times \dfrac{1}{2} =$

8) $\dfrac{3}{2} \times \dfrac{3}{5} =$

9) $\dfrac{3}{2} \times \dfrac{2}{4} =$

10) $\dfrac{4}{3} \times \dfrac{2}{3} =$

Multiply the fractions and convert the answers in Decimal form.

1) $\dfrac{1}{2} \times \dfrac{5}{2} =$

2) $\dfrac{2}{3} \times \dfrac{6}{4} =$

3) $\dfrac{2}{3} \times \dfrac{10}{3} =$

4) $\dfrac{2}{4} \times \dfrac{5}{3} =$

5) $\dfrac{2}{3} \times \dfrac{7}{5} =$

6) $\dfrac{3}{2} \times \dfrac{1}{2} =$

7) $\dfrac{16}{5} \times \dfrac{1}{5} =$

8) $\dfrac{5}{2} \times \dfrac{2}{4} =$

9) $\dfrac{10}{3} \times \dfrac{2}{4} =$

10) $\dfrac{14}{5} \times \dfrac{1}{5} =$

Multiply the fractions and convert the answers in Decimal form.

1) $\dfrac{1}{4} \times \dfrac{13}{4} =$

2) $\dfrac{4}{5} \times \dfrac{3}{2} =$

3) $\dfrac{3}{4} \times \dfrac{7}{3} =$

4) $\dfrac{4}{5} \times \dfrac{11}{4} =$

5) $\dfrac{3}{4} \times \dfrac{3}{2} =$

6) $\dfrac{8}{3} \times \dfrac{2}{5} =$

7) $\dfrac{16}{5} \times \dfrac{1}{3} =$

8) $\dfrac{5}{3} \times \dfrac{2}{3} =$

9) $\dfrac{14}{4} \times \dfrac{3}{4} =$

10) $\dfrac{8}{3} \times \dfrac{1}{5} =$

Multiply the fractions and convert the answers in Decimal form.

1) $\dfrac{1}{3} \times \dfrac{3}{2} =$

2) $\dfrac{2}{3} \times \dfrac{11}{5} =$

3) $\dfrac{1}{5} \times \dfrac{7}{2} =$

4) $\dfrac{1}{2} \times \dfrac{9}{5} =$

5) $\dfrac{3}{5} \times \dfrac{15}{4} =$

6) $\dfrac{7}{3} \times \dfrac{1}{2} =$

7) $\dfrac{11}{4} \times \dfrac{1}{2} =$

8) $\dfrac{7}{3} \times \dfrac{2}{5} =$

9) $\dfrac{6}{5} \times \dfrac{2}{3} =$

10) $\dfrac{18}{5} \times \dfrac{4}{5} =$

Multiply the fractions and convert the answers in Decimal form.

1) $\dfrac{2}{5} \times \dfrac{7}{4} =$

2) $\dfrac{1}{2} \times \dfrac{8}{3} =$

3) $\dfrac{1}{2} \times \dfrac{5}{4} =$

4) $\dfrac{2}{3} \times \dfrac{3}{2} =$

5) $\dfrac{4}{5} \times \dfrac{9}{4} =$

6) $\dfrac{7}{5} \times \dfrac{1}{2} =$

7) $\dfrac{13}{5} \times \dfrac{1}{3} =$

8) $\dfrac{14}{5} \times \dfrac{1}{2} =$

9) $\dfrac{5}{2} \times \dfrac{3}{4} =$

10) $\dfrac{14}{4} \times \dfrac{1}{4} =$

Multiply the fractions and convert the answers in Decimal form.

1) $\dfrac{2}{3} \times \dfrac{3}{2} =$

2) $\dfrac{4}{5} \times \dfrac{7}{4} =$

3) $\dfrac{2}{5} \times \dfrac{8}{3} =$

4) $\dfrac{1}{2} \times \dfrac{5}{3} =$

5) $\dfrac{2}{4} \times \dfrac{11}{3} =$

6) $\dfrac{14}{5} \times \dfrac{1}{2} =$

7) $\dfrac{19}{5} \times \dfrac{2}{3} =$

8) $\dfrac{7}{3} \times \dfrac{1}{4} =$

9) $\dfrac{8}{3} \times \dfrac{2}{5} =$

10) $\dfrac{5}{2} \times \dfrac{1}{4} =$

Multiply the fractions and convert the answers in Decimal form.

1) $\dfrac{1}{2} \times \dfrac{5}{2} =$

2) $\dfrac{1}{5} \times \dfrac{8}{3} =$

3) $\dfrac{2}{3} \times \dfrac{7}{2} =$

4) $\dfrac{2}{3} \times \dfrac{11}{5} =$

5) $\dfrac{4}{5} \times \dfrac{5}{2} =$

6) $\dfrac{8}{5} \times \dfrac{2}{4} =$

7) $\dfrac{10}{3} \times \dfrac{1}{5} =$

8) $\dfrac{17}{5} \times \dfrac{2}{3} =$

9) $\dfrac{13}{4} \times \dfrac{1}{2} =$

10) $\dfrac{9}{4} \times \dfrac{1}{3} =$

Multiply the fractions and convert the answers in Decimal form.

1) $\dfrac{1}{3} \times \dfrac{11}{5} =$

2) $\dfrac{1}{5} \times \dfrac{9}{5} =$

3) $\dfrac{1}{2} \times \dfrac{15}{4} =$

4) $\dfrac{2}{3} \times \dfrac{9}{4} =$

5) $\dfrac{4}{5} \times \dfrac{14}{4} =$

6) $\dfrac{10}{4} \times \dfrac{2}{3} =$

7) $\dfrac{7}{5} \times \dfrac{2}{4} =$

8) $\dfrac{4}{3} \times \dfrac{1}{5} =$

9) $\dfrac{9}{4} \times \dfrac{4}{5} =$

10) $\dfrac{6}{4} \times \dfrac{1}{3} =$

Multiply the fractions and convert the answers in Decimal form.

1) $\dfrac{3}{4} \times \dfrac{5}{2} =$

2) $\dfrac{2}{3} \times \dfrac{11}{3} =$

3) $\dfrac{1}{4} \times \dfrac{8}{5} =$

4) $\dfrac{2}{3} \times \dfrac{6}{4} =$

5) $\dfrac{3}{4} \times \dfrac{14}{4} =$

6) $\dfrac{4}{3} \times \dfrac{1}{4} =$

7) $\dfrac{11}{5} \times \dfrac{2}{4} =$

8) $\dfrac{9}{4} \times \dfrac{1}{2} =$

9) $\dfrac{5}{2} \times \dfrac{1}{5} =$

10) $\dfrac{9}{4} \times \dfrac{1}{5} =$

Multiply the fractions and convert the answers in Decimal form.

1) $\dfrac{1}{3} \times \dfrac{9}{5} =$

2) $\dfrac{2}{3} \times \dfrac{4}{3} =$

3) $\dfrac{1}{2} \times \dfrac{5}{3} =$

4) $\dfrac{1}{2} \times \dfrac{5}{2} =$

5) $\dfrac{1}{4} \times \dfrac{5}{3} =$

6) $\dfrac{11}{5} \times \dfrac{3}{4} =$

7) $\dfrac{13}{5} \times \dfrac{1}{3} =$

8) $\dfrac{10}{3} \times \dfrac{1}{4} =$

9) $\dfrac{5}{4} \times \dfrac{2}{5} =$

10) $\dfrac{7}{4} \times \dfrac{2}{5} =$

MULTIPLYING FRACTIONS

Multiply the fractions and convert the answers in Decimal form.

1) $\dfrac{4}{5} \times \dfrac{7}{3} =$

2) $\dfrac{2}{3} \times \dfrac{5}{2} =$

3) $\dfrac{3}{5} \times \dfrac{3}{2} =$

4) $\dfrac{4}{5} \times \dfrac{12}{5} =$

5) $\dfrac{1}{3} \times \dfrac{7}{4} =$

6) $\dfrac{5}{4} \times \dfrac{1}{3} =$

7) $\dfrac{5}{2} \times \dfrac{3}{5} =$

8) $\dfrac{6}{5} \times \dfrac{1}{3} =$

9) $\dfrac{11}{3} \times \dfrac{4}{5} =$

10) $\dfrac{13}{5} \times \dfrac{1}{2} =$

Multiply the fractions and convert the answers in Decimal form.

1) $\dfrac{4}{5} \times \dfrac{7}{2} =$

2) $\dfrac{2}{4} \times \dfrac{3}{2} =$

3) $\dfrac{3}{4} \times \dfrac{4}{3} =$

4) $\dfrac{1}{4} \times \dfrac{5}{2} =$

5) $\dfrac{2}{3} \times \dfrac{12}{5} =$

6) $\dfrac{5}{3} \times \dfrac{1}{2} =$

7) $\dfrac{11}{4} \times \dfrac{3}{4} =$

8) $\dfrac{5}{3} \times \dfrac{2}{3} =$

9) $\dfrac{13}{4} \times \dfrac{1}{4} =$

10) $\dfrac{5}{2} \times \dfrac{2}{3} =$

Multiply the fractions and convert the answers in Decimal form.

1) $\dfrac{1}{2} \times \dfrac{9}{4} =$

2) $\dfrac{2}{4} \times \dfrac{3}{2} =$

3) $\dfrac{1}{2} \times \dfrac{7}{5} =$

4) $\dfrac{1}{3} \times \dfrac{13}{4} =$

5) $\dfrac{1}{2} \times \dfrac{17}{5} =$

6) $\dfrac{4}{3} \times \dfrac{4}{5} =$

7) $\dfrac{7}{4} \times \dfrac{2}{4} =$

8) $\dfrac{17}{5} \times \dfrac{1}{3} =$

9) $\dfrac{19}{5} \times \dfrac{1}{5} =$

10) $\dfrac{13}{5} \times \dfrac{2}{5} =$

Multiply the fractions and convert the answers in Decimal form.

1) $\dfrac{1}{2} \times \dfrac{11}{3} =$

2) $\dfrac{1}{3} \times \dfrac{10}{4} =$

3) $\dfrac{1}{2} \times \dfrac{15}{4} =$

4) $\dfrac{3}{4} \times \dfrac{5}{3} =$

5) $\dfrac{4}{5} \times \dfrac{5}{2} =$

6) $\dfrac{11}{4} \times \dfrac{2}{4} =$

7) $\dfrac{10}{3} \times \dfrac{2}{3} =$

8) $\dfrac{7}{2} \times \dfrac{2}{5} =$

9) $\dfrac{15}{4} \times \dfrac{1}{2} =$

10) $\dfrac{3}{2} \times \dfrac{4}{5} =$

Multiply the fractions and convert the answers in Decimal form.

1) $\dfrac{3}{5} \times \dfrac{5}{2} =$

2) $\dfrac{1}{4} \times \dfrac{5}{4} =$

3) $\dfrac{1}{2} \times \dfrac{3}{2} =$

4) $\dfrac{1}{3} \times \dfrac{4}{3} =$

5) $\dfrac{1}{2} \times \dfrac{13}{5} =$

6) $\dfrac{11}{3} \times \dfrac{1}{2} =$

7) $\dfrac{4}{3} \times \dfrac{2}{4} =$

8) $\dfrac{5}{2} \times \dfrac{3}{4} =$

9) $\dfrac{16}{5} \times \dfrac{3}{5} =$

10) $\dfrac{15}{4} \times \dfrac{1}{4} =$

Multiply the fractions and convert the answers in Decimal form.

1) $\dfrac{3}{4} \times \dfrac{5}{2} =$

2) $\dfrac{1}{4} \times \dfrac{4}{3} =$

3) $\dfrac{2}{4} \times \dfrac{3}{2} =$

4) $\dfrac{1}{3} \times \dfrac{8}{5} =$

5) $\dfrac{1}{5} \times \dfrac{17}{5} =$

6) $\dfrac{3}{2} \times \dfrac{2}{3} =$

7) $\dfrac{10}{3} \times \dfrac{1}{3} =$

8) $\dfrac{13}{4} \times \dfrac{1}{2} =$

9) $\dfrac{6}{5} \times \dfrac{1}{2} =$

10) $\dfrac{10}{3} \times \dfrac{1}{4} =$

Multiply the fractions and convert the answers in Decimal form.

1) $\dfrac{1}{4} \times \dfrac{7}{2} =$

2) $\dfrac{1}{4} \times \dfrac{3}{2} =$

3) $\dfrac{2}{3} \times \dfrac{14}{5} =$

4) $\dfrac{1}{2} \times \dfrac{3}{2} =$

5) $\dfrac{1}{3} \times \dfrac{11}{5} =$

6) $\dfrac{5}{2} \times \dfrac{1}{5} =$

7) $\dfrac{12}{5} \times \dfrac{3}{5} =$

8) $\dfrac{7}{5} \times \dfrac{2}{4} =$

9) $\dfrac{6}{5} \times \dfrac{2}{5} =$

10) $\dfrac{6}{4} \times \dfrac{2}{5} =$

Multiply the fractions and convert the answers in Decimal form.

1) $\dfrac{1}{4} \times \dfrac{5}{2} =$

2) $\dfrac{1}{4} \times \dfrac{5}{3} =$

3) $\dfrac{1}{2} \times \dfrac{9}{5} =$

4) $\dfrac{1}{5} \times \dfrac{11}{3} =$

5) $\dfrac{3}{5} \times \dfrac{7}{4} =$

6) $\dfrac{11}{4} \times \dfrac{2}{4} =$

7) $\dfrac{3}{2} \times \dfrac{1}{2} =$

8) $\dfrac{5}{2} \times \dfrac{2}{4} =$

9) $\dfrac{7}{3} \times \dfrac{3}{5} =$

10) $\dfrac{8}{3} \times \dfrac{2}{3} =$

Multiply the fractions and convert the answers in Decimal form.

1) $\dfrac{3}{4} \times \dfrac{10}{4} =$

2) $\dfrac{1}{2} \times \dfrac{11}{3} =$

3) $\dfrac{3}{4} \times \dfrac{14}{5} =$

4) $\dfrac{1}{4} \times \dfrac{7}{5} =$

5) $\dfrac{3}{5} \times \dfrac{5}{2} =$

6) $\dfrac{3}{2} \times \dfrac{1}{3} =$

7) $\dfrac{11}{5} \times \dfrac{1}{4} =$

8) $\dfrac{6}{4} \times \dfrac{3}{4} =$

9) $\dfrac{8}{3} \times \dfrac{2}{3} =$

10) $\dfrac{14}{5} \times \dfrac{2}{3} =$

Multiply the fractions and convert the answers in Decimal form.

1) $\dfrac{3}{4} \times \dfrac{10}{3} =$

2) $\dfrac{2}{5} \times \dfrac{8}{5} =$

3) $\dfrac{2}{5} \times \dfrac{6}{5} =$

4) $\dfrac{1}{2} \times \dfrac{8}{3} =$

5) $\dfrac{2}{3} \times \dfrac{6}{4} =$

6) $\dfrac{9}{4} \times \dfrac{2}{3} =$

7) $\dfrac{16}{5} \times \dfrac{1}{5} =$

8) $\dfrac{8}{5} \times \dfrac{4}{5} =$

9) $\dfrac{5}{3} \times \dfrac{2}{3} =$

10) $\dfrac{3}{2} \times \dfrac{2}{3} =$

DIVIDING FRACTIONS

Divide the fractions and convert the answers in Decimal form.

Divide the fractions and convert the answers in Decimal form.

1) $\dfrac{2}{3} \div \dfrac{1}{2} =$

2) $\dfrac{1}{2} \div \dfrac{1}{4} =$

3) $\dfrac{2}{3} \div \dfrac{1}{2} =$

4) $\dfrac{3}{4} \div \dfrac{2}{3} =$

5) $\dfrac{1}{3} \div \dfrac{3}{4} =$

6) $\dfrac{1}{2} \div \dfrac{2}{4} =$

7) $\dfrac{2}{3} \div \dfrac{1}{4} =$

8) $\dfrac{1}{4} \div \dfrac{2}{5} =$

9) $\dfrac{1}{2} \div \dfrac{1}{3} =$

10) $\dfrac{3}{5} \div \dfrac{2}{4} =$

Divide the fractions and convert the answers in Decimal form.

1) $\dfrac{1}{2} \div \dfrac{1}{4} =$

2) $\dfrac{1}{2} \div \dfrac{2}{5} =$

3) $\dfrac{1}{4} \div \dfrac{1}{2} =$

4) $\dfrac{1}{3} \div \dfrac{1}{2} =$

5) $\dfrac{1}{4} \div \dfrac{2}{5} =$

6) $\dfrac{3}{5} \div \dfrac{2}{4} =$

7) $\dfrac{3}{4} \div \dfrac{1}{2} =$

8) $\dfrac{1}{3} \div \dfrac{1}{5} =$

9) $\dfrac{1}{3} \div \dfrac{1}{5} =$

10) $\dfrac{1}{2} \div \dfrac{3}{5} =$

Divide the fractions and convert the answers in Decimal form.

1) $\dfrac{1}{4} \div \dfrac{1}{3} =$

2) $\dfrac{1}{5} \div \dfrac{1}{3} =$

3) $\dfrac{2}{3} \div \dfrac{1}{2} =$

4) $\dfrac{2}{4} \div \dfrac{4}{5} =$

5) $\dfrac{2}{3} \div \dfrac{4}{5} =$

6) $\dfrac{1}{2} \div \dfrac{1}{3} =$

7) $\dfrac{2}{3} \div \dfrac{1}{4} =$

8) $\dfrac{1}{2} \div \dfrac{1}{3} =$

9) $\dfrac{4}{5} \div \dfrac{3}{4} =$

10) $\dfrac{1}{2} \div \dfrac{1}{3} =$

Divide the fractions and convert the answers in Decimal form.

1) $\dfrac{2}{3} \div \dfrac{1}{2} =$

2) $\dfrac{1}{3} \div \dfrac{1}{2} =$

3) $\dfrac{1}{2} \div \dfrac{3}{5} =$

4) $\dfrac{1}{3} \div \dfrac{2}{5} =$

5) $\dfrac{3}{4} \div \dfrac{1}{3} =$

6) $\dfrac{1}{2} \div \dfrac{2}{3} =$

7) $\dfrac{1}{5} \div \dfrac{1}{2} =$

8) $\dfrac{1}{2} \div \dfrac{3}{4} =$

9) $\dfrac{1}{5} \div \dfrac{1}{2} =$

10) $\dfrac{1}{2} \div \dfrac{1}{4} =$

Divide the fractions and convert the answers in Decimal form.

1) $\dfrac{1}{2} \div \dfrac{3}{5} =$

2) $\dfrac{1}{2} \div \dfrac{3}{4} =$

3) $\dfrac{1}{2} \div \dfrac{1}{5} =$

4) $\dfrac{1}{3} \div \dfrac{1}{2} =$

5) $\dfrac{1}{3} \div \dfrac{2}{5} =$

6) $\dfrac{1}{2} \div \dfrac{4}{5} =$

7) $\dfrac{1}{2} \div \dfrac{3}{4} =$

8) $\dfrac{3}{4} \div \dfrac{2}{3} =$

9) $\dfrac{2}{4} \div \dfrac{1}{2} =$

10) $\dfrac{3}{4} \div \dfrac{1}{2} =$

DIVIDING FRACTIONS

ACTIVITY NO: **6**

Divide the fractions and convert the answers in Decimal form.

1) $\dfrac{1}{3} \div \dfrac{1}{2} =$

2) $\dfrac{1}{5} \div \dfrac{3}{4} =$

3) $\dfrac{3}{5} \div \dfrac{1}{2} =$

4) $\dfrac{2}{3} \div \dfrac{1}{2} =$

5) $\dfrac{1}{2} \div \dfrac{2}{3} =$

6) $\dfrac{3}{4} \div \dfrac{1}{2} =$

7) $\dfrac{2}{3} \div \dfrac{2}{5} =$

8) $\dfrac{2}{4} \div \dfrac{2}{5} =$

9) $\dfrac{1}{3} \div \dfrac{1}{4} =$

10) $\dfrac{1}{2} \div \dfrac{1}{4} =$

Divide the fractions and convert the answers in Decimal form.

1) $\dfrac{3}{5} \div \dfrac{1}{2} =$

2) $\dfrac{2}{3} \div \dfrac{1}{2} =$

3) $\dfrac{1}{2} \div \dfrac{2}{3} =$

4) $\dfrac{1}{2} \div \dfrac{1}{3} =$

5) $\dfrac{3}{5} \div \dfrac{1}{3} =$

6) $\dfrac{1}{2} \div \dfrac{2}{5} =$

7) $\dfrac{3}{5} \div \dfrac{3}{4} =$

8) $\dfrac{1}{2} \div \dfrac{1}{3} =$

9) $\dfrac{1}{3} \div \dfrac{1}{5} =$

10) $\dfrac{3}{5} \div \dfrac{1}{2} =$

Divide the fractions and convert the answers in Decimal form.

1) $\dfrac{1}{2} \div \dfrac{2}{3} =$

2) $\dfrac{1}{2} \div \dfrac{3}{4} =$

3) $\dfrac{2}{3} \div \dfrac{2}{4} =$

4) $\dfrac{1}{3} \div \dfrac{3}{4} =$

5) $\dfrac{1}{2} \div \dfrac{1}{3} =$

6) $\dfrac{2}{4} \div \dfrac{2}{3} =$

7) $\dfrac{1}{3} \div \dfrac{3}{5} =$

8) $\dfrac{1}{3} \div \dfrac{3}{4} =$

9) $\dfrac{1}{3} \div \dfrac{1}{2} =$

10) $\dfrac{2}{3} \div \dfrac{1}{4} =$

Divide the fractions and convert the answers in Decimal form.

1) $\dfrac{1}{5} \div \dfrac{1}{3} =$

2) $\dfrac{2}{3} \div \dfrac{3}{4} =$

3) $\dfrac{1}{2} \div \dfrac{3}{4} =$

4) $\dfrac{1}{2} \div \dfrac{3}{4} =$

5) $\dfrac{1}{2} \div \dfrac{1}{5} =$

6) $\dfrac{1}{5} \div \dfrac{2}{3} =$

7) $\dfrac{4}{5} \div \dfrac{2}{3} =$

8) $\dfrac{2}{4} \div \dfrac{1}{2} =$

9) $\dfrac{2}{4} \div \dfrac{2}{5} =$

10) $\dfrac{1}{2} \div \dfrac{3}{5} =$

Divide the fractions and convert the answers in Decimal form.

1) $\dfrac{1}{4} \div \dfrac{4}{5} =$

2) $\dfrac{3}{5} \div \dfrac{1}{2} =$

3) $\dfrac{3}{4} \div \dfrac{2}{3} =$

4) $\dfrac{1}{4} \div \dfrac{1}{2} =$

5) $\dfrac{1}{3} \div \dfrac{2}{4} =$

6) $\dfrac{2}{5} \div \dfrac{1}{4} =$

7) $\dfrac{1}{2} \div \dfrac{2}{3} =$

8) $\dfrac{3}{5} \div \dfrac{1}{2} =$

9) $\dfrac{2}{4} \div \dfrac{2}{5} =$

10) $\dfrac{1}{2} \div \dfrac{1}{5} =$

Divide the fractions and convert the answers in Decimal form.

1) $\dfrac{1}{4} \div \dfrac{1}{3} =$

2) $\dfrac{1}{2} \div \dfrac{1}{5} =$

3) $\dfrac{1}{5} \div \dfrac{3}{4} =$

4) $\dfrac{1}{2} \div \dfrac{1}{3} =$

5) $\dfrac{1}{2} \div \dfrac{1}{4} =$

6) $\dfrac{1}{2} \div \dfrac{2}{4} =$

7) $\dfrac{1}{3} \div \dfrac{2}{4} =$

8) $\dfrac{2}{3} \div \dfrac{2}{4} =$

9) $\dfrac{4}{5} \div \dfrac{3}{4} =$

10) $\dfrac{1}{4} \div \dfrac{2}{5} =$

Divide the fractions and convert the answers in Decimal form.

1) $\dfrac{2}{4} \div \dfrac{1}{5} =$

2) $\dfrac{2}{4} \div \dfrac{3}{5} =$

3) $\dfrac{1}{2} \div \dfrac{4}{5} =$

4) $\dfrac{4}{5} \div \dfrac{1}{4} =$

5) $\dfrac{2}{4} \div \dfrac{1}{2} =$

6) $\dfrac{3}{4} \div \dfrac{1}{5} =$

7) $\dfrac{1}{3} \div \dfrac{1}{5} =$

8) $\dfrac{2}{5} \div \dfrac{1}{4} =$

9) $\dfrac{2}{3} \div \dfrac{1}{5} =$

10) $\dfrac{2}{4} \div \dfrac{1}{3} =$

Divide the fractions and convert the answers in Decimal form.

1) $\dfrac{1}{2} \div \dfrac{1}{5} =$

2) $\dfrac{2}{3} \div \dfrac{1}{2} =$

3) $\dfrac{2}{3} \div \dfrac{1}{5} =$

4) $\dfrac{2}{4} \div \dfrac{4}{5} =$

5) $\dfrac{2}{4} \div \dfrac{1}{2} =$

6) $\dfrac{1}{3} \div \dfrac{1}{2} =$

7) $\dfrac{1}{3} \div \dfrac{2}{4} =$

8) $\dfrac{3}{4} \div \dfrac{2}{5} =$

9) $\dfrac{1}{4} \div \dfrac{1}{2} =$

10) $\dfrac{2}{5} \div \dfrac{1}{2} =$

Divide the fractions and convert the answers in Decimal form.

1) $\dfrac{3}{5} \div \dfrac{2}{4} =$

2) $\dfrac{1}{2} \div \dfrac{2}{3} =$

3) $\dfrac{1}{3} \div \dfrac{3}{4} =$

4) $\dfrac{1}{3} \div \dfrac{2}{4} =$

5) $\dfrac{1}{2} \div \dfrac{1}{3} =$

6) $\dfrac{1}{2} \div \dfrac{2}{8} =$

7) $\dfrac{1}{5} \div \dfrac{1}{2} =$

8) $\dfrac{1}{2} \div \dfrac{3}{4} =$

9) $\dfrac{1}{2} \div \dfrac{3}{4} =$

10) $\dfrac{4}{5} \div \dfrac{1}{2} =$

Divide the fractions and convert the answers in Decimal form.

1) $\dfrac{2}{3} \div \dfrac{1}{4} =$

2) $\dfrac{2}{3} \div \dfrac{2}{4} =$

3) $\dfrac{1}{3} \div \dfrac{1}{2} =$

4) $\dfrac{3}{5} \div \dfrac{1}{3} =$

5) $\dfrac{1}{3} \div \dfrac{1}{2} =$

6) $\dfrac{1}{3} \div \dfrac{1}{4} =$

7) $\dfrac{2}{3} \div \dfrac{1}{2} =$

8) $\dfrac{2}{4} \div \dfrac{4}{5} =$

9) $\dfrac{3}{5} \div \dfrac{1}{3} =$

10) $\dfrac{2}{4} \div \dfrac{1}{2} =$

Divide the fractions and convert the answers in Decimal form.

1) $\dfrac{1}{4} \div \dfrac{2}{5} =$

2) $\dfrac{2}{3} \div \dfrac{1}{5} =$

3) $\dfrac{3}{4} \div \dfrac{1}{4} =$

4) $\dfrac{1}{3} \div \dfrac{1}{5} =$

5) $\dfrac{1}{5} \div \dfrac{2}{4} =$

6) $\dfrac{1}{3} \div \dfrac{1}{2} =$

7) $\dfrac{3}{4} \div \dfrac{1}{2} =$

8) $\dfrac{1}{2} \div \dfrac{3}{4} =$

9) $\dfrac{4}{5} \div \dfrac{1}{3} =$

10) $\dfrac{1}{3} \div \dfrac{2}{5} =$

Divide the fractions and convert the answers in Decimal form.

1) $\dfrac{1}{2} \div \dfrac{2}{4} =$

2) $\dfrac{3}{5} \div \dfrac{2}{3} =$

3) $\dfrac{2}{4} \div \dfrac{1}{2} =$

4) $\dfrac{1}{2} \div \dfrac{1}{4} =$

5) $\dfrac{3}{5} \div \dfrac{2}{4} =$

6) $\dfrac{2}{3} \div \dfrac{4}{5} =$

7) $\dfrac{1}{4} \div \dfrac{1}{2} =$

8) $\dfrac{3}{4} \div \dfrac{2}{5} =$

9) $\dfrac{1}{3} \div \dfrac{1}{2} =$

10) $\dfrac{2}{3} \div \dfrac{2}{4} =$

Divide the fractions and convert the answers in Decimal form.

1) $\dfrac{1}{4} \div \dfrac{2}{3} =$

2) $\dfrac{2}{4} \div \dfrac{1}{2} =$

3) $\dfrac{2}{5} \div \dfrac{1}{2} =$

4) $\dfrac{1}{2} \div \dfrac{2}{3} =$

5) $\dfrac{1}{4} \div \dfrac{3}{5} =$

6) $\dfrac{2}{3} \div \dfrac{3}{5} =$

7) $\dfrac{1}{3} \div \dfrac{3}{4} =$

8) $\dfrac{1}{3} \div \dfrac{2}{4} =$

9) $\dfrac{1}{4} \div \dfrac{1}{5} =$

10) $\dfrac{1}{2} \div \dfrac{3}{4} =$

DIVIDING FRACTIONS

Divide the fractions and convert the answers in Decimal form.

1) $\dfrac{1}{4} \div \dfrac{1}{2} =$

2) $\dfrac{4}{5} \div \dfrac{1}{4} =$

3) $\dfrac{3}{4} \div \dfrac{1}{2} =$

4) $\dfrac{4}{5} \div \dfrac{3}{4} =$

5) $\dfrac{1}{2} \div \dfrac{3}{5} =$

6) $\dfrac{1}{2} \div \dfrac{3}{4} =$

4) $\dfrac{4}{5} \div \dfrac{3}{4} =$

5) $\dfrac{1}{2} \div \dfrac{3}{5} =$

6) $\dfrac{1}{2} \div \dfrac{3}{4} =$

7) $\dfrac{1}{3} \div \dfrac{1}{5} =$

8) $\dfrac{3}{4} \div \dfrac{1}{5} =$

9) $\dfrac{3}{4} \div \dfrac{2}{3} =$

10) $\dfrac{1}{2} \div \dfrac{2}{4} =$

Divide the fractions and convert the answers in Decimal form.

1) $\dfrac{1}{3} \div \dfrac{1}{2} =$

2) $\dfrac{2}{3} \div \dfrac{4}{5} =$

3) $\dfrac{2}{4} \div \dfrac{1}{2} =$

4) $\dfrac{1}{3} \div \dfrac{1}{4} =$

5) $\dfrac{3}{5} \div \dfrac{1}{4} =$

6) $\dfrac{1}{5} \div \dfrac{2}{3} =$

7) $\dfrac{3}{4} \div \dfrac{2}{3} =$

8) $\dfrac{3}{5} \div \dfrac{2}{3} =$

9) $\dfrac{1}{5} \div \dfrac{2}{4} =$

10) $\dfrac{1}{4} \div \dfrac{1}{2} =$

ANSWERS

MULTIPYING FRACTIONS

1) $\frac{3}{5} \times \frac{7}{2} = 2.1$

2) $\frac{2}{4} \times \frac{5}{2} = 1.25$

3) $\frac{2}{3} \times \frac{11}{3} = 2.444$

4) $\frac{1}{2} \times \frac{7}{4} = 0.875$

5) $\frac{1}{2} \times \frac{11}{4} = 1.375$

6) $\frac{8}{5} \times \frac{3}{4} = 1.2$

7) $\frac{14}{5} \times \frac{1}{2} = 1.4$

8) $\frac{3}{2} \times \frac{3}{5} = 0.9$

9) $\frac{3}{2} \times \frac{2}{4} = 0.75$

10) $\frac{4}{3} \times \frac{2}{3} = 0.889$

1) $\frac{1}{2} \times \frac{5}{2} = 0.5$

2) $\frac{2}{3} \times \frac{6}{4} = 1$

3) $\frac{2}{3} \times \frac{10}{3} = 2.222$

4) $\frac{2}{4} \times \frac{5}{3} = 0.833$

5) $\frac{2}{3} \times \frac{7}{5} = 0.933$

6) $\frac{3}{2} \times \frac{1}{2} = 0.75$

7) $\frac{16}{5} \times \frac{1}{5} = 0.64$

8) $\frac{5}{2} \times \frac{2}{4} = 1.25$

9) $\frac{10}{3} \times \frac{2}{4} = 1.667$

10) $\frac{14}{5} \times \frac{1}{5} = 0.56$

FRACTIONS TO DECIMALS — ACTIVITY NO: 3

1) $\frac{1}{4} \times \frac{13}{4} = 0.812$

2) $\frac{4}{5} \times \frac{3}{2} = 1.2$

3) $\frac{3}{4} \times \frac{7}{3} = 1.75$

4) $\frac{4}{5} \times \frac{11}{4} = 2.2$

5) $\frac{3}{4} \times \frac{3}{2} = 1.125$

6) $\frac{8}{3} \times \frac{2}{5} = 1.067$

7) $\frac{16}{5} \times \frac{1}{3} = 1.066$

8) $\frac{5}{3} \times \frac{2}{3} = 1.111$

9) $\frac{14}{4} \times \frac{3}{4} = 2.625$

10) $\frac{8}{3} \times \frac{1}{5} = 0.533$

FRACTIONS TO DECIMALS — ACTIVITY NO: 4

1) $\frac{1}{3} \times \frac{3}{2} = 0.5$

2) $\frac{2}{3} \times \frac{11}{5} = 1.466$

3) $\frac{1}{5} \times \frac{7}{2} = 0.7$

4) $\frac{1}{2} \times \frac{9}{5} = 0.9$

5) $\frac{3}{5} \times \frac{15}{4} = 2.25$

6) $\frac{7}{3} \times \frac{1}{2} = 1.166$

7) $\frac{11}{4} \times \frac{1}{2} = 1.375$

8) $\frac{7}{3} \times \frac{2}{5} = 0.933$

9) $\frac{6}{5} \times \frac{2}{3} = 0.8$

10) $\frac{18}{5} \times \frac{4}{5} = 2.88$

FRACTIONS TO DECIMALS — ACTIVITY NO: 5

1) $\frac{2}{5} \times \frac{7}{4} = 0.7$

2) $\frac{1}{2} \times \frac{8}{3} = 1.333$

3) $\frac{1}{2} \times \frac{5}{4} = 0.625$

4) $\frac{2}{3} \times \frac{3}{2} = 1$

5) $\frac{4}{5} \times \frac{9}{4} = 1.8$

6) $\frac{7}{5} \times \frac{1}{2} = 0.7$

7) $\frac{13}{5} \times \frac{1}{3} = 0.866$

8) $\frac{14}{5} \times \frac{1}{2} = 1.4$

9) $\frac{5}{2} \times \frac{3}{4} = 1.875$

10) $\frac{14}{4} \times \frac{1}{4} = 0.875$

FRACTIONS TO DECIMALS — ACTIVITY NO: 6

1) $\frac{2}{3} \times \frac{3}{2} = 1$

2) $\frac{4}{5} \times \frac{7}{4} = 1.4$

3) $\frac{2}{5} \times \frac{8}{3} = 1.066$

4) $\frac{1}{2} \times \frac{5}{3} = 0.833$

5) $\frac{2}{4} \times \frac{11}{3} = 1.833$

6) $\frac{14}{5} \times \frac{1}{2} = 1.4$

7) $\frac{19}{5} \times \frac{2}{3} = 2.533$

8) $\frac{7}{3} \times \frac{1}{4} = 0.583$

9) $\frac{8}{3} \times \frac{2}{5} = 1.066$

10) $\frac{5}{2} \times \frac{1}{4} = 0.625$

FRACTIONS TO DECIMALS — ACTIVITY NO: 7

1) $\frac{1}{2} \times \frac{5}{2} =$ 1.25
2) $\frac{1}{5} \times \frac{8}{3} =$ 0.533
3) $\frac{2}{3} \times \frac{7}{2} =$ 2.333
4) $\frac{2}{3} \times \frac{11}{5} =$ 1.466
5) $\frac{4}{5} \times \frac{5}{2} =$ 2
6) $\frac{8}{5} \times \frac{2}{4} =$ 0.8
7) $\frac{10}{3} \times \frac{1}{5} =$ 0.666
8) $\frac{17}{5} \times \frac{2}{3} =$ 2.266
9) $\frac{13}{4} \times \frac{1}{2} =$ 1.625
10) $\frac{9}{4} \times \frac{1}{3} =$ 0.75

FRACTIONS TO DECIMALS — ACTIVITY NO: 8

1) $\frac{1}{3} \times \frac{11}{5} =$ 0.733
2) $\frac{1}{5} \times \frac{9}{5} =$ 0.36
3) $\frac{1}{2} \times \frac{15}{4} =$ 0.625
4) $\frac{2}{3} \times \frac{9}{4} =$ 1.5
5) $\frac{4}{5} \times \frac{14}{4} =$ 2.8
6) $\frac{10}{4} \times \frac{2}{3} =$ 1.666
7) $\frac{7}{5} \times \frac{2}{4} =$ 0.7
8) $\frac{4}{3} \times \frac{1}{5} =$ 0.266
9) $\frac{9}{4} \times \frac{4}{5} =$ 1.8
10) $\frac{6}{4} \times \frac{1}{3} =$ 0.5

FRACTIONS TO DECIMALS — ACTIVITY NO: 9

1) $\frac{3}{4} \times \frac{5}{2} =$ 1.875
2) $\frac{2}{3} \times \frac{11}{3} =$ 2.444
3) $\frac{1}{4} \times \frac{8}{5} =$ 0.4
4) $\frac{2}{3} \times \frac{6}{4} =$ 1
5) $\frac{3}{4} \times \frac{14}{4} =$ 2.625
6) $\frac{4}{3} \times \frac{1}{4} =$ 0.333
7) $\frac{11}{5} \times \frac{2}{4} =$ 1.1
8) $\frac{9}{4} \times \frac{1}{2} =$ 1.125
9) $\frac{5}{2} \times \frac{1}{5} =$ 0.5
10) $\frac{9}{4} \times \frac{1}{5} =$ 0.45

FRACTIONS TO DECIMALS — ACTIVITY NO: 10

1) $\frac{1}{3} \times \frac{9}{5} =$ 0.6
2) $\frac{2}{3} \times \frac{4}{3} =$ 0.888
3) $\frac{1}{2} \times \frac{5}{3} =$ 0.833
4) $\frac{1}{2} \times \frac{5}{2} =$ 1.25
5) $\frac{1}{4} \times \frac{5}{3} =$ 0.416
6) $\frac{11}{5} \times \frac{3}{4} =$ 1.65
7) $\frac{13}{5} \times \frac{1}{3} =$ 0.866
8) $\frac{10}{3} \times \frac{1}{4} =$ 0.833
9) $\frac{5}{4} \times \frac{2}{5} =$ 0.5
10) $\frac{7}{4} \times \frac{2}{5} =$ 0.7

1) $\dfrac{4}{5} \times \dfrac{7}{3} =$ 1.867
2) $\dfrac{2}{3} \times \dfrac{5}{2} =$ 1.666
3) $\dfrac{3}{5} \times \dfrac{3}{2} =$ 0.9
4) $\dfrac{4}{5} \times \dfrac{12}{5} =$ 1.92
5) $\dfrac{1}{3} \times \dfrac{7}{4} =$ 0.583
6) $\dfrac{5}{4} \times \dfrac{1}{3} =$ 0.416
7) $\dfrac{5}{2} \times \dfrac{3}{5} =$ 1.5
8) $\dfrac{6}{5} \times \dfrac{1}{3} =$ 0.4
9) $\dfrac{11}{3} \times \dfrac{4}{5} =$ 2.93
10) $\dfrac{13}{5} \times \dfrac{1}{2} =$ 1.3

1) $\dfrac{4}{5} \times \dfrac{7}{2} =$ 2.8
2) $\dfrac{2}{4} \times \dfrac{3}{2} =$ 0.75
3) $\dfrac{3}{4} \times \dfrac{4}{3} =$ 1
4) $\dfrac{1}{4} \times \dfrac{5}{2} =$ 0.625
5) $\dfrac{2}{3} \times \dfrac{12}{5} =$ 1.6
6) $\dfrac{5}{3} \times \dfrac{1}{2} =$ 0.833
7) $\dfrac{11}{4} \times \dfrac{3}{4} =$ 2.062
8) $\dfrac{5}{3} \times \dfrac{2}{3} =$ 1.111
9) $\dfrac{13}{4} \times \dfrac{1}{4} =$ 0.812
10) $\dfrac{5}{2} \times \dfrac{2}{3} =$ 1.666

1) $\dfrac{1}{2} \times \dfrac{9}{4} =$ 1.125
2) $\dfrac{2}{4} \times \dfrac{3}{2} =$ 0.75
3) $\dfrac{1}{2} \times \dfrac{7}{5} =$ 0.7
4) $\dfrac{1}{3} \times \dfrac{13}{4} =$ 1.083
5) $\dfrac{1}{2} \times \dfrac{17}{5} =$ 1.7
6) $\dfrac{4}{3} \times \dfrac{4}{5} =$ 1.066
7) $\dfrac{7}{4} \times \dfrac{2}{4} =$ 0.875
8) $\dfrac{17}{5} \times \dfrac{1}{3} =$ 1.133
9) $\dfrac{19}{5} \times \dfrac{1}{5} =$ 0.76
10) $\dfrac{13}{5} \times \dfrac{2}{5} =$ 1.04

1) $\dfrac{1}{2} \times \dfrac{11}{3} =$ 1.833
2) $\dfrac{1}{3} \times \dfrac{10}{4} =$ 0.833
3) $\dfrac{1}{2} \times \dfrac{15}{4} =$ 1.875
4) $\dfrac{3}{4} \times \dfrac{5}{3} =$ 1.25
5) $\dfrac{4}{5} \times \dfrac{5}{2} =$ 2
6) $\dfrac{11}{4} \times \dfrac{2}{4} =$ 1.375
7) $\dfrac{10}{3} \times \dfrac{2}{3} =$ 2.222
8) $\dfrac{7}{2} \times \dfrac{2}{5} =$ 1.4
9) $\dfrac{15}{4} \times \dfrac{1}{2} =$ 1.875
10) $\dfrac{3}{2} \times \dfrac{4}{5} =$ 1.2

COMPARISON OF DECIMALS AND FRACTIONS — ACTIVITY NO: 15

1) $\frac{3}{5} \times \frac{5}{2} = 1.5$
2) $\frac{1}{4} \times \frac{5}{4} = 0.312$
3) $\frac{1}{2} \times \frac{3}{2} = 0.75$
4) $\frac{1}{3} \times \frac{4}{3} = 0.444$
5) $\frac{1}{2} \times \frac{13}{5} = 1.3$
6) $\frac{11}{3} \times \frac{1}{2} = 1.833$
7) $\frac{4}{3} \times \frac{2}{4} = 0.666$
8) $\frac{5}{2} \times \frac{3}{4} = 1.875$
9) $\frac{16}{5} \times \frac{3}{5} = 1.92$
10) $\frac{15}{4} \times \frac{1}{4} = 0.937$

COMPARISON OF DECIMALS AND FRACTIONS — ACTIVITY NO: 16

1) $\frac{3}{4} \times \frac{5}{2} = 1.875$
2) $\frac{1}{4} \times \frac{4}{3} = 0.333$
3) $\frac{2}{4} \times \frac{3}{2} = 0.75$
4) $\frac{1}{3} \times \frac{8}{5} = 0.533$
5) $\frac{1}{5} \times \frac{17}{5} = 0.68$
6) $\frac{3}{2} \times \frac{2}{3} = 1$
7) $\frac{10}{3} \times \frac{1}{3} = 1.111$
8) $\frac{13}{4} \times \frac{1}{2} = 1.625$
9) $\frac{6}{5} \times \frac{1}{2} = 0.6$
10) $\frac{10}{3} \times \frac{1}{4} = 0.833$

COMPARISON OF DECIMALS AND FRACTIONS — ACTIVITY NO: 17

1) $\frac{1}{4} \times \frac{7}{2} = 0.875$
2) $\frac{1}{4} \times \frac{3}{2} = 0.375$
3) $\frac{2}{3} \times \frac{14}{5} = 1.866$
4) $\frac{1}{2} \times \frac{3}{2} = 0.75$
5) $\frac{1}{3} \times \frac{11}{5} = 0.733$
6) $\frac{5}{2} \times \frac{1}{5} = 0.5$
7) $\frac{12}{5} \times \frac{3}{5} = 1.44$
8) $\frac{7}{5} \times \frac{2}{4} = 0.7$
9) $\frac{6}{5} \times \frac{2}{5} = 0.48$
10) $\frac{6}{4} \times \frac{2}{5} = 0.6$

COMPARISON OF DECIMALS AND FRACTIONS — ACTIVITY NO: 18

1) $\frac{1}{4} \times \frac{5}{2} = 0.625$
2) $\frac{1}{4} \times \frac{5}{3} = 0.416$
3) $\frac{1}{2} \times \frac{9}{5} = 0.9$
4) $\frac{1}{5} \times \frac{11}{3} = 0.733$
5) $\frac{3}{5} \times \frac{7}{4} = 1.05$
6) $\frac{11}{4} \times \frac{2}{4} = 1.375$
7) $\frac{3}{2} \times \frac{1}{2} = 0.75$
8) $\frac{5}{2} \times \frac{2}{4} = 1.25$
9) $\frac{7}{3} \times \frac{3}{5} = 1.4$
10) $\frac{8}{3} \times \frac{2}{3} = 1.777$

1) $\frac{3}{4} \times \frac{10}{4} = 1.875$

2) $\frac{1}{2} \times \frac{11}{3} = 1.833$

3) $\frac{3}{4} \times \frac{14}{5} = 2.1$

4) $\frac{1}{4} \times \frac{7}{5} = 0.35$

5) $\frac{3}{5} \times \frac{5}{2} = 1.5$

6) $\frac{3}{2} \times \frac{1}{3} = 0.5$

7) $\frac{11}{5} \times \frac{1}{4} = 0.55$

8) $\frac{6}{4} \times \frac{3}{4} = 1.125$

9) $\frac{8}{3} \times \frac{2}{3} = 1.777$

10) $\frac{14}{5} \times \frac{2}{3} = 1.866$

1) $\frac{3}{4} \times \frac{10}{3} = 2.5$

2) $\frac{2}{5} \times \frac{8}{5} = 0.64$

3) $\frac{2}{5} \times \frac{6}{5} = 0.48$

4) $\frac{1}{2} \times \frac{8}{3} = 1.333$

5) $\frac{2}{3} \times \frac{6}{4} = 1$

6) $\frac{9}{4} \times \frac{2}{3} = 1.5$

7) $\frac{16}{5} \times \frac{1}{5} = 0.64$

8) $\frac{8}{5} \times \frac{4}{5} = 1.28$

9) $\frac{5}{3} \times \frac{2}{3} = 1.111$

10) $\frac{3}{2} \times \frac{2}{3} = 1$

DIVIDING FRACTIONS

Activity No: 1 — DECIMALS TO FRACTIONS

1) $\frac{2}{3} \div \frac{1}{2} = 0.333$

2) $\frac{1}{2} \div \frac{1}{4} = 0.125$

3) $\frac{2}{3} \div \frac{1}{2} = 0.133$

4) $\frac{3}{4} \div \frac{2}{3} = 0.125$

5) $\frac{1}{3} \div \frac{3}{4} = 0.027$

6) $\frac{1}{2} \div \frac{2}{4} = 0.062$

7) $\frac{2}{3} \div \frac{1}{4} = 0.166$

8) $\frac{1}{4} \div \frac{2}{5} = 0.025$

9) $\frac{1}{2} \div \frac{1}{3} = 0.166$

10) $\frac{3}{5} \div \frac{2}{4} = 0.075$

Activity No: 2 — DECIMALS TO FRACTIONS

1) $\frac{1}{2} \div \frac{1}{4} = 0.125$

2) $\frac{1}{2} \div \frac{2}{5} = 0.05$

3) $\frac{1}{4} \div \frac{1}{2} = 0.125$

4) $\frac{1}{3} \div \frac{1}{2} = 0.166$

5) $\frac{1}{4} \div \frac{2}{5} = 0.025$

6) $\frac{3}{5} \div \frac{2}{4} = 0.075$

7) $\frac{3}{4} \div \frac{1}{2} = 0.375$

8) $\frac{1}{3} \div \frac{1}{5} = 0.06$

9) $\frac{1}{3} \div \frac{1}{5} = 0.066$

10) $\frac{1}{2} \div \frac{3}{5} = 0.066$

1) $\frac{1}{4} \div \frac{1}{3} = 0.083$
2) $\frac{1}{5} \div \frac{1}{3} = 0.066$
3) $\frac{2}{3} \div \frac{1}{2} = 0.333$
4) $\frac{2}{4} \div \frac{4}{5} = 0.025$
5) $\frac{2}{3} \div \frac{4}{5} = 0.033$
6) $\frac{1}{2} \div \frac{1}{3} = 0.166$
7) $\frac{2}{3} \div \frac{1}{4} = 0.166$
8) $\frac{1}{2} \div \frac{1}{3} = 0.166$
9) $\frac{4}{5} \div \frac{3}{4} = 0.066$
10) $\frac{1}{2} \div \frac{1}{3} = 0.166$

1) $\frac{2}{3} \div \frac{1}{2} = 0.333$
2) $\frac{1}{3} \div \frac{1}{2} = 0.166$
3) $\frac{1}{2} \div \frac{3}{5} = 0.033$
4) $\frac{1}{3} \div \frac{2}{5} = 0.033$
5) $\frac{3}{4} \div \frac{1}{3} = 0.25$
6) $\frac{1}{2} \div \frac{2}{3} = 0.083$
7) $\frac{1}{5} \div \frac{1}{2} = 0.1$
8) $\frac{1}{2} \div \frac{3}{4} = 0.041$
9) $\frac{1}{5} \div \frac{1}{2} = 0.1$
10) $\frac{1}{2} \div \frac{1}{4} = 0.041$

1) $\frac{1}{2} \div \frac{3}{5} = 0.033$
2) $\frac{1}{2} \div \frac{3}{4} = 0.041$
3) $\frac{1}{2} \div \frac{1}{5} = 0.1$
4) $\frac{1}{3} \div \frac{1}{2} = 0.166$
5) $\frac{1}{3} \div \frac{2}{5} = 0.033$
6) $\frac{1}{2} \div \frac{4}{5} = 0.025$
7) $\frac{1}{2} \div \frac{3}{4} = 0.041$
8) $\frac{3}{4} \div \frac{2}{3} = 0.125$
9) $\frac{2}{4} \div \frac{1}{2} = 0.25$
10) $\frac{3}{4} \div \frac{1}{2} = 0.375$

1) $\frac{1}{3} \div \frac{1}{2} = 0.166$
2) $\frac{1}{5} \div \frac{3}{4} = 0.016$
3) $\frac{3}{5} \div \frac{1}{2} = 0.3$
4) $\frac{2}{3} \div \frac{1}{2} = 0.333$
5) $\frac{1}{2} \div \frac{2}{3} = 0.083$
6) $\frac{3}{4} \div \frac{1}{2} = 0.375$
7) $\frac{2}{3} \div \frac{2}{5} = 0.066$
8) $\frac{2}{4} \div \frac{2}{5} = 0.05$
9) $\frac{1}{3} \div \frac{1}{4} = 0.083$
10) $\frac{1}{2} \div \frac{1}{4} = 0.125$

1) $\frac{3}{5} \div \frac{1}{2} = 0.3$
2) $\frac{2}{3} \div \frac{1}{2} = 0.333$
3) $\frac{1}{2} \div \frac{2}{3} = 0.083$
4) $\frac{1}{2} \div \frac{1}{3} = 0.166$
5) $\frac{3}{5} \div \frac{1}{3} = 0.2$
6) $\frac{1}{2} \div \frac{2}{5} = 0.05$
7) $\frac{3}{5} \div \frac{3}{4} = 0.05$
8) $\frac{1}{2} \div \frac{1}{3} = 0.166$
9) $\frac{1}{3} \div \frac{1}{5} = 0.033$
10) $\frac{3}{5} \div \frac{1}{2} = 0.3$

1) $\frac{1}{2} \div \frac{2}{3} = 0.083$
2) $\frac{1}{2} \div \frac{3}{4} = 0.041$
3) $\frac{2}{3} \div \frac{2}{4} = 0.083$
4) $\frac{1}{3} \div \frac{3}{4} = 0.027$
5) $\frac{1}{2} \div \frac{1}{3} = 0.166$
6) $\frac{2}{4} \div \frac{2}{3} = 0.083$
7) $\frac{1}{3} \div \frac{3}{5} = 0.022$
8) $\frac{1}{3} \div \frac{3}{4} = 0.027$
9) $\frac{1}{3} \div \frac{1}{2} = 0.166$
10) $\frac{2}{3} \div \frac{1}{4} = 0.166$

1) $\frac{1}{5} \div \frac{1}{3} = 0.066$
2) $\frac{2}{3} \div \frac{3}{4} = 0.055$
3) $\frac{1}{2} \div \frac{3}{4} = 0.041$
4) $\frac{1}{2} \div \frac{3}{4} = 0.041$
5) $\frac{1}{2} \div \frac{1}{5} = 0.1$
6) $\frac{1}{5} \div \frac{2}{3} = 0.033$
7) $\frac{4}{5} \div \frac{2}{3} = 0.133$
8) $\frac{2}{4} \div \frac{1}{2} = 0.1$
9) $\frac{2}{4} \div \frac{2}{5} = 0.05$
10) $\frac{1}{2} \div \frac{3}{5} = 0.033$

1) $\frac{1}{4} \div \frac{4}{5} = 0.012$
2) $\frac{3}{5} \div \frac{1}{2} = 0.3$
3) $\frac{3}{4} \div \frac{2}{3} = 0.125$
4) $\frac{1}{4} \div \frac{1}{2} = 0.125$
5) $\frac{1}{3} \div \frac{2}{4} = 0.041$
6) $\frac{2}{5} \div \frac{1}{4} = 0.1$
7) $\frac{1}{2} \div \frac{2}{3} = 0.083$
8) $\frac{3}{5} \div \frac{1}{2} = 0.3$
9) $\frac{2}{4} \div \frac{2}{5} = 0.05$
10) $\frac{1}{2} \div \frac{1}{5} = 0.1$

COMPARISON OF DECIMALS AND FRACTIONS — ACTIVITY NO: 11

1) $\frac{1}{4} \div \frac{1}{3} = 0.083$
2) $\frac{1}{2} \div \frac{1}{5} = 0.1$
3) $\frac{1}{5} \div \frac{3}{4} = 0.017$
4) $\frac{1}{2} \div \frac{1}{3} = 0.166$
5) $\frac{1}{2} \div \frac{1}{4} = 0.125$
6) $\frac{1}{2} \div \frac{2}{4} = 0.063$
7) $\frac{1}{3} \div \frac{2}{4} = 0.042$
8) $\frac{2}{3} \div \frac{2}{4} = 0.083$
9) $\frac{4}{5} \div \frac{3}{4} = 0.067$
10) $\frac{1}{4} \div \frac{2}{5} = 0.025$

COMPARISON OF DECIMALS AND FRACTIONS — ACTIVITY NO: 12

1) $\frac{2}{4} \div \frac{1}{5} = 0.1$
2) $\frac{2}{4} \div \frac{3}{5} = 0.033$
3) $\frac{1}{2} \div \frac{4}{5} = 0.025$
4) $\frac{4}{5} \div \frac{1}{4} = 0.2$
5) $\frac{2}{4} \div \frac{1}{2} = 0.25$
6) $\frac{3}{4} \div \frac{1}{5} = 0.15$
7) $\frac{1}{3} \div \frac{1}{5} = 0.066$
8) $\frac{2}{5} \div \frac{1}{4} = 0.1$
9) $\frac{2}{3} \div \frac{1}{5} = 0.133$
10) $\frac{2}{4} \div \frac{1}{3} = 0.166$

COMPARISON OF DECIMALS AND FRACTIONS — ACTIVITY NO: 13

1) $\frac{1}{2} \div \frac{1}{5} = 0.1$
2) $\frac{2}{3} \div \frac{1}{2} = 0.333$
3) $\frac{2}{3} \div \frac{1}{5} = 0.133$
4) $\frac{2}{4} \div \frac{4}{5} = 0.025$
5) $\frac{2}{4} \div \frac{1}{2} = 0.25$
6) $\frac{1}{3} \div \frac{1}{2} = 0.166$
7) $\frac{1}{3} \div \frac{2}{4} = 0.041$
8) $\frac{3}{4} \div \frac{2}{5} = 0.075$
9) $\frac{1}{4} \div \frac{1}{2} = 0.125$
10) $\frac{2}{5} \div \frac{1}{2} = 0.2$

COMPARISON OF DECIMALS AND FRACTIONS — ACTIVITY NO: 14

1) $\frac{3}{5} \div \frac{2}{4} = 0.075$
2) $\frac{1}{2} \div \frac{2}{3} = 0.083$
3) $\frac{1}{3} \div \frac{3}{4} = 0.027$
4) $\frac{1}{3} \div \frac{2}{4} = 0.041$
5) $\frac{1}{2} \div \frac{1}{3} = 0.166$
6) $\frac{1}{2} \div \frac{2}{8} = 0.031$
7) $\frac{1}{5} \div \frac{1}{2} = 0.1$
8) $\frac{1}{2} \div \frac{3}{4} = 0.041$
9) $\frac{1}{2} \div \frac{3}{4} = 0.041$
10) $\frac{4}{5} \div \frac{1}{2} = 0.4$

COMPARISON OF DECIMALS AND FRACTIONS — ACTIVITY NO: 15

1) $\frac{2}{3} \div \frac{1}{4} = 0.166$
2) $\frac{2}{3} \div \frac{2}{4} = 0.083$
3) $\frac{1}{3} \div \frac{1}{2} = 0.166$
4) $\frac{3}{5} \div \frac{1}{3} = 0.15$
5) $\frac{1}{3} \div \frac{1}{2} = 0.166$
6) $\frac{1}{3} \div \frac{1}{4} = 0.083$
7) $\frac{2}{3} \div \frac{1}{2} = 0.333$
8) $\frac{2}{4} \div \frac{4}{5} = 0.025$
9) $\frac{3}{5} \div \frac{1}{3} = 0.2$
10) $\frac{2}{4} \div \frac{1}{2} = 0.25$

COMPARISON OF DECIMALS AND FRACTIONS — ACTIVITY NO: 16

1) $\frac{1}{4} \div \frac{2}{5} = 0.025$
2) $\frac{2}{3} \div \frac{1}{5} = 0.133$
3) $\frac{3}{4} \div \frac{1}{4} = 0.187$
4) $\frac{1}{3} \div \frac{1}{5} = 0.066$
5) $\frac{1}{5} \div \frac{2}{4} = 0.025$
6) $\frac{1}{3} \div \frac{1}{2} = 0.166$
7) $\frac{3}{4} \div \frac{1}{2} = 0.375$
8) $\frac{1}{2} \div \frac{3}{4} = 0.041$
9) $\frac{4}{5} \div \frac{1}{3} = 0.266$
10) $\frac{1}{3} \div \frac{2}{5} = 0.033$

COMPARISON OF DECIMALS AND FRACTIONS — ACTIVITY NO: 17

1) $\frac{1}{2} \div \frac{2}{4} = 0.063$
2) $\frac{3}{5} \div \frac{2}{3} = 0.1$
3) $\frac{2}{4} \div \frac{1}{2} = 0.25$
4) $\frac{1}{2} \div \frac{1}{4} = 0.125$
5) $\frac{3}{5} \div \frac{2}{4} = 0.075$
6) $\frac{2}{3} \div \frac{4}{5} = 0.033$
7) $\frac{1}{4} \div \frac{1}{2} = 0.125$
8) $\frac{3}{4} \div \frac{2}{5} = 0.075$
9) $\frac{1}{3} \div \frac{1}{2} = 0.166$
10) $\frac{2}{3} \div \frac{2}{4} = 0.083$

COMPARISON OF DECIMALS AND FRACTIONS — ACTIVITY NO: 18

1) $\frac{1}{4} \div \frac{2}{3} = 0.042$
2) $\frac{2}{4} \div \frac{1}{2} = 0.25$
3) $\frac{2}{5} \div \frac{1}{2} = 0.2$
4) $\frac{1}{2} \div \frac{2}{3} = 0.083$
5) $\frac{1}{4} \div \frac{3}{5} = 0.017$
6) $\frac{2}{3} \div \frac{3}{5} = 0.044$
7) $\frac{1}{3} \div \frac{3}{4} = 0.027$
8) $\frac{1}{3} \div \frac{2}{4} = 0.042$
9) $\frac{1}{4} \div \frac{1}{5} = 0.05$
10) $\frac{1}{2} \div \frac{3}{4} = 0.042$

1) $\frac{1}{4} \div \frac{1}{2} = 0.125$

2) $\frac{4}{5} \div \frac{1}{4} = 0.2$

3) $\frac{3}{4} \div \frac{1}{2} = 0.375$

4) $\frac{4}{5} \div \frac{3}{4} = 0.067$

5) $\frac{1}{2} \div \frac{3}{5} = 0.033$

6) $\frac{1}{2} \div \frac{3}{4} = 0.041$

7) $\frac{1}{3} \div \frac{1}{5} = 0.066$

8) $\frac{3}{4} \div \frac{1}{5} = 0.15$

9) $\frac{3}{4} \div \frac{2}{3} = 0.125$

10) $\frac{1}{2} \div \frac{2}{4} = 0.063$

1) $\frac{1}{3} \div \frac{1}{2} = 0.166$

2) $\frac{2}{3} \div \frac{4}{5} = 0.033$

3) $\frac{2}{4} \div \frac{1}{2} = 0.25$

4) $\frac{1}{3} \div \frac{1}{4} = 0.083$

5) $\frac{3}{5} \div \frac{1}{4} = 0.15$

6) $\frac{1}{5} \div \frac{2}{3} = 0.033$

7) $\frac{3}{4} \div \frac{2}{3} = 0.125$

8) $\frac{3}{5} \div \frac{2}{3} = 0.1$

9) $\frac{1}{5} \div \frac{2}{4} = 0.025$

10) $\frac{1}{4} \div \frac{1}{2} = 0.125$

Visit

BABY PROFESSOR
EDUCATION KIDS

www.BabyProfessorBooks.com
to download Free Baby Professor eBooks
and view our catalog of new and exciting
Children's Books

www.ingramcontent.com/pod-product-compliance
Lightning Source LLC
Chambersburg PA
CBHW080759120726
48001CB00009B/2806